# I HAVE PRAYED SINCE "THEN"

## Living Without Guilt Through the Power of Prayer

M. Ruth Thomas

ISBN 978-1-941749-79-1
LCCN 2018950626
4-P Publishing

# Contents

# ABOUT THE AUTHOR

Ruth Thomas is the President and Founder of Real Life Christian Ministries, Inc., and A Remnant Ministries, Chattanooga, Tennessee. As a child, Ruth experienced sexual and emotional abuse and as a result, spent most of her life longing to be accepted and loved by others. She felt she had to prove that she was worthy of acceptance. Ruth made many mistakes in life that caused her to live with guilt. The beginning of her freedom from past mistakes came during one of her prayer times when she read Luke 4:18 in the Amplified Bible:

> The Spirit of the Lord [is] upon Me, because He has **anointed Me [the Anointed One, the messiah] to** preach the good news [the Gospel] to the poor; He has sent Me to announce release to the captives and recovery of sight to the blind, to send forth as delivered those who are oppressed [who are downtrodden, bruised, crushed, and broken down by calamity].

Ruth started on her new journey of letting go of the past which included constant renewing of her mind to think and see herself as God saw her – free and delivered! Life circumstances and interactions with others were barriers to further growth until an unpleasant conversation resulted in a paradigm shift in which Ruth heard words that would forever change her life, "I have prayed since then." This new mantra coupled with the power of Luke 4:18 became a part of her life toolkit that manifested in her freedom. Ruth desires to see others free from living with guilt through prayer and applying God's Word in every circumstance.

In this book, Ruth openly shares her journey to freedom along with others who "have prayed since then." She is a conference speaker and host of A Kingdom Gathering where she teaches how to live a kingdom life regardless of circumstances. She is also the host of A Kingdom Word radio broadcast, heard weekly on WNOO, 1260 AM in Chattanooga.

Ruth can be contacted at (423) 899-2552 or mrthomas1950@gmail.com

# DEDICATION

"But when He, the Spirit of Truth (the Truth-giving
Spirit) comes, He will guide you into all the Truth (the
whole, full Truth). For He will not speak His own
message [on His own authority]; but He will tell
whatever He hears [from the Father; He will give the
message that has been given to Him], and He will
announce and declare to you the things that are to
come [that will happen in the future]."
**(John 16:13)**

My story is dedicated to the Holy Spirit, the Spirit of Truth. During a crucial and painful moment in my life – a time when I was feeling guilty about my past mistakes – I heard the Holy Spirit say, "You have prayed since then." I distinctly heard this in my spirit. I experienced a release from the past and peace I had not previously encountered. I had changed, and He reminded me of that change; a change that had occurred because of my surrendering to the Word of God and having a lifestyle of prayer.

To Him alone, I dedicate this story and my life.

M. Ruth Thomas

# ACKNOWLEDGEMENTS

**My Coach, Mrs. Laura Brown, S.W.A.T Book Camp**

I am thankful God placed you in my life. My dream is now a reality because you took your lessons learned and developed an awesome book camp. Thanks, Coach, for believing in me and being patient through my many questions and moments of doubt.

**My Editor, Dr. Jennifer Elizabeth Brunton**

I believe we both agree that God divinely put us together. Thanks for the markups and feedback. Thanks for your brutal honesty. We are just beginning. I love you.

**Life Experiences (The Good, the Bad, and the Ugly)**

WOW, I would not be writing if not for my life experiences! God used them to reveal the painful truths of my heart and to show me a more excellent way to rise and shine. I was often embarrassed by what was revealed, but - more importantly - I was empowered by God's Word and prayer to declare: I HAVE PRAYED SINCE "THEN." It doesn't matter what life brings me, I know assuredly that the Greater One lives in me and His Holy Spirit will never leave me nor forsake me.

# INTRODUCTION

The two-fold purpose of this book is to aid you, the reader, in being set free from the age-old feeling of guilt stemming from past mistakes (your "thens," made because of where you were at that time in life) and to demonstrate the benefits of having a lifestyle of prayer. I am writing as a believer in Christ Jesus, sharing my experiences of living a painful life because of guilt for many years and of how God's Word and prayer changed my life about this negative feeling.

Over our lifetimes, we are going to experience many "thens." In my definition, your "thens" are the mess ups in your life, the things you wish you had not said or done and cannot change. You want to erase it all, but it is too late. And the worst part is the reminders – people's memories and the sad fact that they do not easily let you forget. You are constantly reminded of your "thens" as if you are the only one in the world who has them. Hey, you know what I am talking about. Not only has it happened to me – people keeping me in my past - but I have been guilty of doing the same to others. I desire that you, dear reader, will embrace the power of prayer and experience freedom from living with guilt. In order to show you how this is possible, I will begin with some personal history.

# PROLOGUE

Behold, I was brought forth in [a state of] iniquity; my mother was sinful who conceived me [and I too am sinful].
**(Psalm 51:5)**

I was born because of my mother's adulterous affair. I was a middle child. I can recall as early as five years of age hearing Momma telling me that I would never be any good. It seemed she was dead set on punishing me because she got caught. She would often say:

- You are not capable of being loved.
- Your husband and kids will never love you.
- You are nothing but a bitch.
- You will never amount to anything.

These and many other degrading words were spoken to me for many years. The person who should have built me up tore me down. As a result, I spent most of my life with a feeling of unworthiness. She put me out of her house when I was sixteen years of age. I have been on my own in the 50-plus years since then.

I was determined to prove her wrong as I went on my way, yet I had no life model. I was left to figure life out alone. I made so many mistakes as an individual. I later married and had children. Sadly, as my life went on, Momma's words seemed to be true. I was a classic example of a dysfunctional person.

My decisions and actions were a result of inner pain. I was trying to prove my mother wrong, trying to show her, myself, and others that I was worthy of being loved. My dysfunctional roots were deep and caused me to spend most of my life in a proving mode that resulted in causing hurt to others whom I loved. I lived with guilt for years.

For example, I recall experiencing a difficult situation at work. I had a friend who pulled me out of my situation and gave me a position on her staff. It was a position that afforded me an opportunity to move up in the company. Her superior was impressed with my performance and began to deal directly with me, leaving my friend out of important discussions. My dysfunctional roots caused me to ignore what she had done for me because I finally felt important! I was needed! I was respected by a senior officer! I did not consider that my friend was the one who hired me and who also had the authority to reverse her decision - which is exactly what she did. I loved her, but I hurt her. I didn't prove anything; instead, I manifested Momma's words of being unworthy.

It was many years later that I shared where I was emotionally during that time and asked my friend to forgive me. I am confident that she forgave me, but it was also clear that we would not have a relationship. There are consequences to everything we do, and this was my consequence – forgiven but not forgotten.

So, when I speak of my "thens" I am speaking of true things that I did or said because of where I was during this time of need-iness, a period during which I felt a constant sense of failure.

I reference the Word of God throughout this book because I am a strong believer in its power when applied to life circum-stances. I want you to experience this same power. Here is how the Word of God began to manifest itself in my "then" dysfunctional life of guilt, need, and failure.

My new life began during the winter of 1976, when my hus-band and I visited a local church on a Friday night. I remember it was a cool and pleasant evening. I was pregnant with our third child. As I listened to the preacher talk about Jesus and how much He loved us and came to save us, I felt an emptiness. I thought to myself about how Momma had betrayed love – both marital love and love for her child – and wondered how Jesus could love me as this preacher was describing. Would He betray me? Would He really help me? The preacher was so passionate about this Jesus.

The loving Jesus he described was not the Jesus I learned about in the Baptist church I attended as a child. My memory was of a

Jesus who was distant and sort of mean. He did not care if you lived right or not; just come to church every time the doors opened.

The passion of this "new" Jesus caused my blood to rush quickly through my body. I felt a warmth inside that I couldn't explain. At that moment, I knew I had to connect with this Jesus. My heart was anxious for the preacher to finish his sermon so that I could make my way to the altar. Oh, how I recall that moment in my life. When the preacher invited those who wanted Jesus to come down, I rushed to the altar before Jesus could change His mind. On some level, I feared He might be influenced by what Momma had said about me and decide that I wasn't worthy of Him.

I say this was the start of my new life because the preacher primarily focused on salvation. Of course, that is what I needed - but I also needed to be delivered from my past. As a result, I went on in life still behaving in dysfunctional ways. From that moment of salvation on, though — and this was my saving grace - I began reading the Bible and praying because the preacher said the Word of God and prayer were very important. I wanted to know this Jesus for myself. I wanted to know why He felt I was so important when my own Momma didn't.

I didn't know any special way to pray. I simply talked to Jesus as if He was sitting in the chair across from me. There were times of laughter but, more importantly, my spirit became less heavy by His love. He allowed me to share my hurts. I never felt embarrassed; I felt happy because He listened to me. He was waiting for me when I would wake up at 3 a.m. because I felt He was saying "come and be with Me." As I was learning about Him, I was also learning about myself. In this way, my dysfunctional roots were eventually replaced with the functional roots of His Spirit and His Word.

My Mother passed in 2018. Because of prayer and God's Word, I had forgiven her long before her death. I know she did things because of her experiences and the pain she suffered. Although she never apologized to me or made any effort to know me, I had compassion for her. I am thankful that she no longer physically suffers. Perhaps, we will see each other in another place and time.

Yes, my reader, I have prayed since "then." Let's go on. And by the way, I use "thens" and mistakes interchangeably.

# FOUNDATION

If the foundations are destroyed, what can the [unyieldingly] righteous do, or what has He [the Righteous One] wrought or accomplished?
**(Psalms 11:3)**

But he who merely hears and does not practice doing My words is like a man who built a house on the ground without a foundation, against which the torrent burst, and immediately it collapsed and fell, and the breaking and ruin of that house was great.
**(Luke 6:49)**

For no other foundation can anyone lay than that which is [already] laid, which is Jesus Christ (the Messiah, the Anointed One).
**(I Corinthians 3:11)**

For he was [waiting expectantly and confidently] looking forward to the city which has fixed and firm foundations, whose Architect and Builder is God.
**(Hebrews 11:10)**

My dear reader, before I share about true guilt, it is important for me to explain why I did and said things that harmed myself as well as others. My words and actions resulted from something that is known by a big word: They arose from my "foundation." I shared some about my foundation in the Prologue and will say more in the beginning of the chapter on true guilt. However, I believe it is important for your freedom that I discuss foundations in more detail.

Dear reader, what you are about to read was painful for me to write, and it will be painful for you to take in. But there is liberation in opening the door on great suffering, as healing can also come in through that opening.

My objective is to provide an understanding of the impact our foundations have on our actions. I believe this understanding will empower you to both address your foundation and replace it with God's Word. I have provided a few Scriptures to aid you in having a real foundation.

Noah Webster's 1828 dictionary defines foundation as "the basis or ground-work of anything; that on which anything stands, and by which it is supported."

My basis and ground-work began with the fact that my family was very poor. I have often said that if one defined poor, it would be my family. My five siblings and I lived in a one-bedroom house on the east side of town with momma and daddy. Three additional siblings were born later.

Momma was beautiful and caught the attention of men wherever she was. Daddy was a weak man in that he was unable to stand up enough for himself to have a mutually respectful relationship with momma, and thus she did whatever she desired. Our lives evolved around her. For example, she would often have fresh meat for dinner while we ate beans or potted meat. She said the doctor wanted her to eat quality meat. We were children and didn't know any better. When things didn't go her way, she would pretend to pass out to engage our sympathy – and it worked for years. She seemed to always win (whatever that meant to her).

Momma and daddy both grew up poor and during a time when promiscuousness was an "unspoken" way of life. It was not uncommon for parents to engage in sexual encounters with their children. That was my parents' foundation.

Daddy was extremely light-skinned. Momma was brown-skinned with long hair. I look exactly like her. No one thought it strange that all of the White kids were light-skinned except little Mattie (me)! Momma was glad because the neighbor's words, "Mattie looks just like you," softened her guilt. Momma knew daddy was not my biological father.

I recall being five years old and watching daddy leave to catch the bus for work. One of momma's boyfriends would then arrive, like clockwork. They would have their sexual encounter, making me watch from start to finish. In addition to the negative words she said to me (see Prologue), she would tell me that she knew I wanted what was in her boyfriend's pants. She would then do sexual things to me that a child should never experience. This experience, coupled with her daily emotional abuse, lasted many years.

I was told that I was nothing and incapable of being loved by anyone. I was only worth the pleasure of her sexual and emotional abuse. Momma's sexual abuse eventually stopped, but the damage had been done – and it profoundly shaped my dysfunctional life. Her emotional abuse never stopped even after she put me out of the house as a young girl.

She seemed to look for ways to punish me. For example, I recall a painful experience from elementary school. I desperately needed to go to the restroom but my teacher would not permit it.

22

I tried to explain my desperation but she remained unrelenting and instructed me to wait until I went home. The school was within walking distance from home and I walked as fast as I could, squeezing every muscle but I was unsuccessful. I walked in the door carrying the odor of my accident. I began to explain to momma that my teacher would not allow me to go to the restroom. Momma nonetheless took a switch and beat me until my legs bled. She reminded me of how worthless I was. My foundation was clear – I deserved every punishment that came my way - even when I was innocent. And parallel to believing this, I also felt a need to prove myself. Oh my, proving became a major part of my foundation that lasted well into my senior years.

My destructive foundation caused me to do and say things that caused hurt to me and others. I learned that neediness breeds deception. I lived a deceptive and hypocritical life by pretending to be happy. Externally, I presented an image of perfection because I needed to prove I had my life together. All a big lie! I lived in an unhappy state most of my life.

OK! Back to me looking like momma and having her skin color. When I was in my early 20s, a gentleman who used to come around our home approached me. Neither my siblings nor I knew that he had been one of momma's boyfriends. He was good looking and a popular person in the city. On this particular day, he asked if I knew who he was. Of course, I remembered him visiting our home when I was a young child. He held up a mirror and instructed me to look in the mirror, specifically at my nose and then to look at his nose. He said, "I am your daddy and I don't want to die without you knowing that." He went on to explain the affair he and momma had engaged in years ago. I looked like momma but had his nose and voice.

In that moment, a sense of excitement and belonging came

23

over me, but it didn't last long. He explained that he was married and told me that we would have to keep our relationship a secret because he did not want to hurt his wife. I had a brother and two sisters by him, and he promised to introduce me if his wife passed before him. She did pass and again I was excited, but I then experienced more rejection when he said he couldn't introduce me because his other children would be disappointed to know he had cheated on their mom.

What about me? Did I matter at all? My foundation – more rejection and abandonment. He had pictures of me as a little girl and well into my adult years. He felt this was vindication of his love for me – but - seriously – where was he when momma abused me? Well, it seemed to me that this was just how life was – at least then, anyway.

I did not have Christ as my foundation as the Scripture advises above. I lived instead on the foundation of the problematic issues of my heart for almost 45 years. My primary issues were rejection and abandonment. I recall the many walks I would take asking God where He was. I would wonder if He saw what I was experiencing. Did He even care? If He was so powerful, why didn't He come and help me? I feel sad writing this, but it was the truth of my heart. I didn't know Him then; however, in time, He used all of my pain and mistakes to shape me into being a vessel of honor, fit for His use.

I want you, dear reader, to understand the pitfalls of operating out of a foundation other than Christ Jesus. You suffer and cause others to suffer as well.

I want to share another example that strengthened my dysfunctional foundation.

In 1964-65 I was nominated to compete for queen of my junior high school class. My speech was taken from Ralph Waldo Emerson's quote, "Hitch your wagon to a star." I also performed a creative dance. I received a standing ovation for my performance. The other girls had parents and friends to cheer them on, but no one was there to cheer me on – I was all alone. I honestly felt I had won the competition, but I didn't win the crown. I came in first place. It was only later that one of the teachers confided that I did in fact win, but they had decided to crown the light- skinned girl instead, although they felt my speech and dance had been incredible. This experience added more pain to my wounded soul. I continued to build on sinking sand well into 1995.

I could share mistake after mistake made because of my former foundation. I pray that you continue to read with an opened heart so God can reveal the truth of your foundation. It took the revealed reality of God's Word for me to replace my old foundation with the fresh foundation of Christ Jesus.

I learned and continue to learn to build on His Word by hearing, receiving and acting on it. Let me provide another Scripture for your meditation:

> Neither is new wine put in old wineskins; for if it is,
> the skins burst and are torn in pieces, and the wine is
> spilled and the skins are ruined. But new wine is put
> into fresh wineskins, and so both are preserved.
> **(Matthew 9:17).**

Dear reader, I respectfully ask that you re-read the definition of foundation and Luke 6:49. My basis or ground-work; that on which I stood and by which I was supported consisted of the problematic issues of my heart. As a result, my old wineskin was bursting until my Divine Heavenly Father rescued me. I have been drinking new wine for 23 years. He wants to rescue you and I pray you will allow Him to do so!

Now, let's read about one other hindrance before we get to my chapter on True Guilt.

# UNCONTROLLED
# EMOTIONS

For I am full of troubles, and my life draws near to Sheol (the place of the dead).
**(Psalm 88:3)**

(25) My earthly life cleaves to the dust; revive and stimulate me according to Your word! (28) My life dissolves and weeps itself away for heaviness; raise me up and strengthen me according to [the promises of] Your word.
**(Psalm 119:25 and 28)**

Look on the right hand [the point of attack] and see; for there is no man who knows me [to appear for me]. Refuge has failed me and I have no way to flee; no man cares for my life or my welfare.
**(Psalm 142:4)**

He who has no rule over his own spirit is like a city that is broken down and without walls.
**(Proverbs 25:28)**

Incline your ear [submit and consent to the divine will] and come to Me; hear, and your soul will revive; and I will make an everlasting covenant or league with you, even the sure mercy (kindness, goodwill, and compassion) promised to David. **(Isaiah 55:3)**

God is a Spirit (a spiritual Being) and those who worship Him must worship Him in spirit and in truth (reality).
**(John 4:24)**

The second hindrance I want to share regards the impact of uncontrolled emotions. I pray that your heart is opened as a result of the above discussion on foundation. My objective for now sharing about uncontrolled emotions is to further nurture the mindset of "I want to be free from living with guilt" before it is time to read about true and false guilt.

The majority of my years were built on the problematic issues of my heart. I did not have control over my emotions. I lived by others' standards in order to be accepted and loved. I was like a city broken down and without walls as stated in Proverbs 25:28. I was driven to prove momma wrong and that caused me to be out of control. The one and only positive side of my uncontrolled emotions was my determination to be better than what momma said I was. Unlike so many whose foundation of pain relegate them to living on public welfare, my pain led to determination – which drove me to work and earn my way in life.

While I easily gravitated toward others' standards, I was also slowly establishing my own. It was those standards that eventually led me to take control of my destiny. I learned and continue to learn to build walls by God's Word and not my emotions.

Now, Noah Webster's 1828 Dictionary defines emotion as "Literally, a moving of the mind or soul; hence, any agitation of mind or excitement of sensibility."

God gave us emotions – He gave us a soul (mind, will, and emotions). I believe that everything God did was good, so I believe emotions are good. I define uncontrolled emotions as **reacting** immediately to situations, as opposed to calmly and rationally processing feelings/situations in order to **respond** objectively.

That same dictionary defines react as, "To return an impulse or impression; to resist the action of another body by an opposite force; to resist any influence or power." Respond is defined as, "To answer; to reply; to correspond."

Because I was governed by problematic issues of my heart, I reacted to every situation that caused me (from my hurt perspective) to feel inadequate. My uncontrolled emotions caused me to do and say irrational things. It seemed like everything caused me to cry or feel inadequate. I was trying so hard to feel adequate and worthy of love and acceptance that any feedback was an attack on my "good" efforts. Ha! When others called me needy, I would retaliate with "you don't know me." And that was true, because I didn't know myself - so how could anyone else know me? I stated earlier that neediness breeds deception. As well as presenting myself in deceptive ways, I was so easily deceived by others. A smile or "good job Ruth" were indicators that I was loved and accepted. I would cling to those who offered praise, only to later learn they had no intention to help me or get to know me.

Today, as a follower of Christ and a Pastor, I do my best to offer what I needed then to those around me – real love and acceptance. I consistently pray for God's leadership to see beyond one's faults/flaws, etc., and determine their real need.

I recall attending a Presbyterian church. The Pastor and his wife seemed to be loving people. Please bear in mind, I am sharing about uncontrolled emotions. I loved being in their presence to the point that I called their home daily, often twice a day or more. I was reacting to their "Ruth, call whenever you need us." Now that is not something you say to a needy person. During one of my daily phone calls, the Pastor's wife instructed me to **STOP** calling. She told me that she was tired of me calling her home every day. I was devastated! Lord, have mercy! I felt so rejected by her. Please don't look for rational thought because I didn't have any. I had no control over my emotions. I allowed her words to add to my already powerful sense of inadequacy. I remember the pastor telling her to

30

apologize to me because she was not expressing love and that I would eventually stop calling. They both were right. I did call too much and yes, the day would come – but it came immediately and not for mature reasons. My uncontrolled emotions prompted me to never call again! I thank God for His mercy.

I learned that uncontrolled emotions caused me – as they do with most of us – to go from one extreme to another. My actions with this pastor and his wife exemplified a lack of stability. I was never in balance about anything. I learned later how to live a balanced life through God's Word and prayer.

My uncontrolled emotions stemming from my dysfunctional foundation caused me to accept emotional and physical abuse from my boyfriend/husband. I share some of our story in the chapter on true guilt. I believe that no one has a right to have psychological control over another person. I gave him control because I was out of control. I also felt I deserved the negative things he did and said to me (trying to prove momma wrong but proving her right). Crazy but true. Of course, he was as dysfunctional as I was. I felt that bearing the things he did and said was my way of demonstrating that I was a good girlfriend/wife – uncontrolled emotions, dear reader.

I want to share something else: Circumstances do not make or break you but reveal the truth of your heart. It has been the continual revelation of truth that has caused me to incline my ear to God and experience kindness, goodwill and compassion. My heart was filled with problematic issues that prompted uncontrolled emotions. I was hurting and regardless of the many churches I attended – no one saw my pain; no one reached out to help me to know Jesus or learn about Him and His provision of deliverance. I was only a number in the congregation. No one looked past my faults to see my needs. I didn't understand what it meant to worship God in spirit and truth.

When God called me to minister His Word, I vowed to Him to be an expression of His love to **everyone** I came in contact with. I am able to minister His love because His love is within my heart. His love replaced my dysfunctional heart. He gave me a heart to reach beyond what I saw (and see) to empower others to rise from their pain to freedom. I bless His Name forever.

I learned how to live in the spirit and respond to situations as opposed to reacting. I want everyone who walks in the doors of my ministry to experience being a person and not a number. I do this by teaching practical application of God's Word.

One of my learned early mantras was: **A WALK IN THE SPIRT IS A WALK OF POWER**.

- Power to obey His Word without compromise or adulteration.
- Power to be free.
- Power to live a balanced life.

Our foundation of problematic issues coupled with our uncontrolled emotions can be brought to an end and we can live, powerfully, in the earth!

OK, let's read about true guilt with a desire for more of Him!

# TRUE GUILT

Confess to one another therefore your faults (your slips, your false steps, your offenses, your sins) and pray [also] for one another, that you may be healed and restored [to a spiritual tone of mind and heart]. The earnest (heartfelt, continued prayer of a righteous man makes tremendous power available [dynamic in its working].
**(James 5:16)**

I believe that our hearts provide the foundation for our behavior. An unhealthy foundation produces unhealthy actions. My foundation entailed the need to feel worthy of love and acceptance. I therefore did and said things that I thought would promote love and acceptance, but those actions and words instead hurt others. In other words, I made mistakes. By "true guilt," I refer to the real mistakes we have made in our lives, actions we are "guilty of" by earthly standards, for which we are both accountable and responsible.

Because I knew I hurt others, I lived with guilt most of my life. However, I received deliverance because of continued prayer, and, years later, coming to understand God's Word. The day came when I was able to confess my mistakes and ask for forgiveness. I was learning to respond to life circumstances from a Biblical perspective.

Although I had changed, others did not easily accept or recognize the change, and continually reminded me of my past behavior. For example, for many years, my family had been accustomed to my throwing their personal belongings away if they were in "my space." I had determined "my" space to be the living room and kitchen. This would drive them crazy, and they would let me know that I had no right to throw their things away. Now, if you are a parent or spouse, or have ever had roommates, I am sure you have communicated many times about putting things where they belong if they are so important. However, because of prayer, I realized that it was wrong to throw things away in that context and I stopped. After all, the living room and kitchen was "our" space, not only mine. It seemed to take forever for my family to realize that I had stopped this behavior. Whenever they could not find something, I would hear, "Why did you throw my stuff away?" Not only did they deem me to be guilty, but I was also still living in guilt. I eventually experienced a release from that feeling of guilt, even as I repeatedly told them that I did not throw things out anymore. Through prayer, I learned that neither I nor anyone else can change the past – and why live with guilt and others' reminders when God is in the present?

Whew, the day finally came when they realized that I had changed! Even so, they would occasionally ask if I had thrown their things away. In some ways, I am not sure if we ever entirely get past our "thens." I do believe, though, that prayer empowers us to move forward and glorify God despite the occasional reminders.

I want to be transparent in sharing my story with you. In the introduction, I mentioned the painful words my Momma said to me as a child. Because of that pain, I sought love that resulted in becoming pregnant at 16. My Momma put me out of our home and I started on a journey for which I was not prepared; a journey that led to countless mistakes as a person and a mother. My husband and I lived together for several years before marriage. He came from a dysfunctional family as well. So, you have two dysfunctional people – you can't imagine! Anyway, James was a man of the world, and I was a needy young girl looking for love. He was street smart, a gambler and hustler. It was clear to him that he had full control of my mind and he used it to his advantage.

I believed everything he said. For example, if he said the moon was brown, it was brown - although it wasn't; whatever James said, was true in my sick thinking. I continued to have children and no model as to how to raise them. As a result, I made mistakes as a mother. I loved my kids very much, but my man/husband was the focus of my life. I tried to be there for my children the best way I knew how. My definition of love was being present, providing a meal and a roof and allowing them to talk to me about any subject.

36

We stressed the need for a formal education because of neither of us having access to that privilege. I was also trying to provide another thing I never had when I was a child – love. Although I perceived my efforts as loving, I was trying to fulfill my needs through them.

The truth was I didn't have any identity on my own. James identified who I was. He decided the clothes I wore and how I responded to life circumstances – all to his benefit. It wasn't until many years later that we both changed, and I became my own person, but by that point, so much damage had been done because neither of us knew how to raise children. For example, my kids needed more than just the basics of life. They needed emotional fortitude – something I didn't have and therefore couldn't give. Despite my mistakes as a Mother, my kids turned out pretty good and I am proud of them.

I lived with guilt for many years because I couldn't provide a more healthy and stable environment for them. But, because of God's Word and prayer, the day came when I forgave myself because God had forgiven me. I now know I can't change my past mistakes and I refuse to allow anyone to keep me in bondage.

If you are a parent who, like me, made mistakes, please forgive yourself as God has forgiven you. Do not allow anyone to hold you to your past. I can't stress this enough. It is pointless and will only keep you in a standing still position – never moving forward. This is spoken from a voice of experience.

I have made mistakes ("thens"), and I will make more. As much as we strive not to have them, "thens" are a part of life. I like to look at it as a part of the process of living. We do not normally intend to cause hurt or disappointment, but - because we are individuals - we sometimes say or do things in the wrong place or with bad timing. Our words and actions may also be misperceived. Our "thens" are often, inescapable, and unavoidable. In my experience, they can be reduced by thinking before speaking, accepting the leadership of the Holy Spirit, and receiving the freedom that comes through Christ Jesus. Unfortunately, we tend to constantly interpret things based on our foundations rather than having mature conversations aimed at truly understanding others' intentions and where they were in life at a given time. Let me explain. During my early years as a believer, I was in the needy position of longing to be accepted by others. While the last desire in my heart was to cause hurt to anyone, I nonetheless did so. Hurt people tend to hurt other people because they are operating out of pain rather than freedom. I said and did things from a "needy" heart.

I recall saying something to someone out of the feeling that it would promote acceptance, but it did not. It caused hurt. I asked for forgiveness but did not receive it. Because I wanted to be accepted and loved, I pleaded for forgiveness - still to no avail. What I received was constant reminders of my mistake. Years later, during prayer one morning, I thought about that situation and realized I could have made a better choice of words or not said anything at all in the first place. The Holy Spirit reminded me of the growth I had experienced because of prayer. The person to whom I had spoken unwisely would often bring up my mistake, but I was finally able to ignore those reminders because I had prayed since "then."

I became a person of prayer starting the day I accepted Christ Jesus as my Savior. I have learned that it is impossible to pray with a pure heart and remain the same. In prayer, I have grown much more than I could have imagined. To this day, I look to my time in prayer to hear the voice of God; His leading, guiding, correcting, and of course, His love. I do not want to live without having a relationship with God.

Most of us want to be viewed as caring and loving people. As born-again believers, we should exemplify the characteristics of Christ in our day to day living and thinking. I believe God uses our circumstances to reveal the truth of our hearts. We cannot demonstrate His character when we have problematic issues within that have not been healed. For example, many years ago, I was the speaker at a friend's ministry. In my "then" immature state I addressed a problem. What I said was Biblically correct, but I addressed the problem incorrectly – by bringing the matter up publicly rather than in private. I thought that I could not let people leave in error, but I should have left the situation alone and trusted God to address it in His time and way. My "then" friend and I had committed never to let anything or anyone separate us. We had vowed to discuss our concerns. That circumstance revealed the truth of both of our hearts – we were both immature. I never heard from her after the meeting.

When I learned why my friend stopped talking to me, I asked for forgiveness and tried to explain my immaturity. I conveyed my desire for her to experience my growth, assuring her that I had honestly prayed and grown since "then." I took full responsibility for my incorrect approach as her speaker, but she chose not to hear me. She was hurt - and concluded that we could no longer have a relationship. As far as I know, she continued her ministry. I do wonder, though, what she teaches about God's love and forgiveness. What does she say to her congregants if they make a mistake (for whatever reason) and then realize their error and confess that they were wrong? Could it be possible that - having prayed since "then" – they do not deserve abandonment because of a mistake?" What about the errors my old friend makes? Should we leave her in "then" based on those mistakes? Certainly not!

I have learned that believers often respond to guilt as if they were imitating the court system. A guilty verdict indicates punishment. In that system, theft may carry a twelve-month sentence for a first-time offender; while murder may result in a life sentence. There are lots of variables determining the appropriate punishment for a given crime. In my experience, believers in Christ also inflict punishment on those of like faith who are deemed guilty of mistakes; yet this is not characteristic of the God I serve!

My friend punished me by not forgiving me of my mistake, by insisting upon indefinite separation and leaving no room for reconciliation. Hey, I think believers are called to a ministry of reconciliation. Let us look at the court system of God's Word:

> **Matthew 18:15-17** reads: (15) If your brother wrongs you, go and show him his fault, between you and him privately. If he listens to you, you have won back your brother. (16) But if he does not listen, take along with you one or two others, so that every word may be confirmed and upheld by the testimony of two or three witnesses. (17) If he pays no attention to them [refusing to listen and obey], tell it to the church; and if he refuses to listen even to the church, let him be to you as a pagan and a tax collector.

> **I Corinthians 6:1-8** reads: (1) Does any of you dare, when he has a matter of complaint against another [brother], to go to law before unrighteous men [men neither upright nor right with God, laying it before them] instead of before the saints (the people of God)? (2) Do you know that the saints (the believers) will [one day] judge and govern the world? And if the world [itself] is to be judged and ruled by you, are you unworthy and incompetent to try [such petty matters] of the smallest courts of justice? (3) Do you not know also that we [Christians] are to judge the [very] angels

and pronounce opinion between right and wrong [for them]? How much more then [as to] matters pertaining to this world and of this life only? [(4)] If then you do have such cases of everyday life to decide, why do you appoint [as judges to lay them before] those who [from the standpoint] of the church count for least and are without standing? [(5)] I say this to move you to shame. Can it be that there is not one man among you who [in action is governed by piety and integrity and] is wise and competent enough to decide [the private grievances, disputes, and quarrels] between members of the brotherhood, [(6)] But brother goes to law against brother, and that before [Gentile judges who are] unbelievers [without faith or trust in the Gospel of Christ]? [(7)] Why, the very fact of your having lawsuits with one another at all is a defect (a defeat, an evidence of positive moral loss for you). Why not rather be cheated (defrauded and robbed)? [(8)] But [instead it is you] yourselves who wrong and defraud, and that even your own brethren [by so treating them]!

If we are not to take one another (believers) to a public court, why would God want us to judge and hold each other endlessly accountable for mistakes? We can understand God's heart by understanding His Word and His intention. He does not want us to judge and offend each other. He does not want us to hold one another to past mistakes. I believe He wants us to be a strength to each other by speaking the truth in love. Let's look at **Romans chapter 14:10-13**

(10) Why do you criticize and pass judgment on your brother? Or you, why do you look down upon or despise your brother? For we shall all stand before the judgment seat of God. (13) Then let us no more criticize and blame and pass judgment on one another, but rather decide and endeavor never to

put a stumbling block or an obstacle or a hindrance in the way of a brother.

Being continuously reminded of our mistakes can be a stumbling block, an obstacle, and an impediment to growth – not to mention a hindrance to fruitful relationships. My prayer is that my old friend and I will someday reconnect and demonstrate God's court system.

I confess that if God treated me as we often treat one another, I would not be writing today. I do not know what I would be doing or even where I would be. At one point in my life, I asked Him if He realized how many mistakes I have made that did not glorify Him. He has a way of covering by pouring His love into our hearts. In my experience, His covering has made me desire Him more and want to grow in His likeness. His covering does not remove the consequences of our faults but reveals more excellent ways to manage them and to avoid repeating the same mistakes.

Therefore, I am a firm believer in prayer and its benefits. I have experienced peace on an ongoing basis - despite consequences. My heavenly Father assures and reassures me that He has not left me and has forgiven me. Oh, my dear reader, please use this tool – I HAVE PRAYED SINCE "THEN." I can only imagine what it would be like if every believer chose to live like Him: How many souls would be saved and transformed? How effective could we be in bringing others to desire the God we serve? I think it is a thought worthy of pondering! I am reminded of **John 8:31-32, 36** which reads:

(31) So Jesus said to those Jews who had believed in Him, If you abide in My word [hold fast to My teachings, and live in accordance with them], you are truly My disciples. (32) And you will know the Truth, and the Truth will set you free. (36) So if the Son liberates you [makes you free men], then you are really and unquestionably free.

It is interesting to note what makes one a disciple. Jesus speaks of abiding in His word and thus knowing the Truth and being free. How many true disciples are there? It is not judgmental to state that we believers and churchgoers need to give serious thought to where we are in our hearts, thoughts, words, and actions as regards His Word. The church is supposed to be powerful; it is supposed to manifest Christ on earth. We cannot do that if we are not abiding in Him. A true disciple is one who follows Christ - not just in words, but in actions.

We are not manifesting Him when we cannot forgive, or when we constantly remind others of the ways they have hurt us. We are supposed to walk in the Spirit and fulfill the works (fruit) of the Spirit and not our flesh. **Galatians 5:22-25** reads:

(22) But the fruit of the Spirit is love, joy, peace, longsuffering, gentleness, goodness, faith, (23) Meekness, temperance: against such there is no law. (24) And they that are Christ's have crucified the flesh with the affections and lusts. (25) If we live in the Spirit, let us also walk in the Spirit.

Hey, church, "Wake up." Judgment begins in the house of God. I Peter 4:8 states: Above all things have intense and unfailing love for one another, for love covers a multitude of sins [forgives and disregards the offenses of others]. I believe that we sometimes do not have prayer power because we do not have love power. God's love in us can cause us to step inside another person's prison to bring them out to experience His power and glory. We need to judge ourselves so no one outside of us can judge (this is also scripturally based). The fruit of the Spirit is NOT reminding others of their mistakes.

God's Word speaks so much about prayer. Jesus was a Man given to prayer. His outward power was a result of His inward prayer. He spent many nights in prayer and came out walking in miraculous power. Many years ago, I knew two very similar individuals. One of them prayed all the time, and the other prayed not at all, yet despite this seemingly major difference, they were doing

43

the same things. Both consistently found fault in others and perceived themselves as almost blameless. My husband explained this situation by saying, "The one who is praying is praying with a made-up mind; God speaks to an opened mind."

It is so important to have a humble heart when seeking God. I often say that it is impossible to have a lifestyle of prayer and stay the same. There is good news here! The individual described above who was praying changed eventually - after choosing to have an opened mind and heart. This person has prayed since "then."

I recall a painful experience that occurred during a prayer group gathering. A brother spoke at length about believers being the righteousness of God and sanctified in Him. He went on and on about the importance of believers knowing who they are in Christ. I responded, that as believers we continue to "say" words without manifesting them in our lives and actions. Non-believers don't need to hear words, they need to witness us demonstrating who we are in Christ – and believers' hearts, too, are bolstered by such witnessing. I further shared that we should be bearing fruit that reflects Christ's Lordship in our lives. Enough talk! Let's live this life. I later found out that he was very upset with me and ended our potential affiliation. I tried to seek peace with him as instructed in the Word of God, but to no avail. But I spoke up because I believe that speech that is not directly and promptly reflected in our actions becomes empty speech – and is thus not a manifestation of Christ living in us. Again, it is impossible to pray with an opened heart and not bear fruit reflective of Christ Jesus.

Jesus was teaching us something by His lifestyle of prayer. I believe He wanted us to understand that prayer brings about personal change and entrance into the Presence of God. I believe He was teaching that prayer causes the manifestation of God's power in our lives and ministries. We pray without ceasing because we realize that we cannot do anything without God's help.

May I ask you to pause for a moment and imagine what you would experience with this type of mindset. Are you willing to have this type of prayerful life? If our minds and hearts are continuously in prayer, we cannot easily judge others and continuously remind them of their mistakes. We know from personal experience that perhaps that person we would have otherwise criticized has prayed since "then." We feel more compassion in response to other people's mistakes.

I love praying and understanding God's Word. I believe His Word should be the guiding principle for day-to-day living. It has been my experience that prayer and applying God's Word increases the presence and influence of the Holy Spirit in one's life. Because of this, I understand what it is to live by the credo, "not my will but Thine be done." I believe the following Scripture supports my perspective. **Luke 11:1-13** reads:

> [1] THEN HE was praying in a certain place; and when He stopped, one of His disciples said to Him, Lord, teach us to pray, [just] as John taught his disciples. [2] And He said to them, When you pray, say: Our Father Who is in heaven, hallowed be Your name, Your kingdom come. Your will be done [held holy and revered] on earth as it is in heaven. [3] Give us daily our daily [bread food for the morrow]. [4] And forgive us our sins, for we ourselves also forgive everyone who is indebted to us [who has offended us or done us wrong]. And bring us not into temptation but rescue us from evil. [5] And he said unto them, Which of you who has a friend will go to him at midnight and will say unto him, Friend, lend me three loaves [of bread], [6] For a friend of mine who is on a journey has just come, and I have nothing to put

before him; (7) And he from within will answe, Do not disturb me; the door is now closed, and my children are with me in bed; I cannot get up and supply you [with anything]? (8) I tell you, although he will get up and supply him anything because he is his friend, yet because of his shameless persistence and insistence he will get up and give him as much as he needs. (9) So, I say to you, Ask and keep on asking and it shall be given you; seek and keep on seeking, and you shall find; knock and keep on knocking, and the door shall be opened to you. (10) For everyone who asks and keeps on asking receives; and he who seeks and keeps on seeking finds; and to him who knocks and keeps on knocking, the door shall be opened. (11) What father among you, if his son asks for a loaf of bread, will give him a stone; or if he asks for a fish, will instead of a fish give him a serpent? (12) Or if he asks an egg, will give him a scorpion? (13) If you then, evil as you are, know how to give good gifts [gifts that are to their advantage]to your children how much more will your heavenly Father give the Holy Spirit to those who ask and continue to ask Him!

Here, Jesus is responding to the disciple's inquiry about prayer. Jesus not only taught his disciples how to pray but revealed the **fruit of prayer** which is an increase of the Holy Spirit (note verse 13). When I first came across this Scripture, I realized how powerful prayer was and is. My heart was longing for more of Christ because I did not want to remain as I was. In my spirit, I would hear phrases like "coming to the end of self." I learned that because I was praying with a desire for more, I was slowly decreasing, while – in a manifestation of Scripture - His Spirit was increasing in me. I praise Him today because I continue to grow and decrease, and His Holy Spirit continues to increase in my heart. I have learned to think (more) before speaking. I have learned the importance of being led by His Spirit and not my thoughts. I continue to learn how to manifest the mind of Christ.

I have also learned to extend mercy to others when they say or do something that hurts me, or they say or do something in error. Each of us speaks from where we are. When challenged, I choose - because of prayer and the Word - to see past the situation rather than bring condemnation to the individual involved. I have learned to seek my Father's will regarding whether He wants me to speak up or to leave things alone and intercede. Sometimes I will see that same person after some time has passed and, noticing changes in them, realize that they, too, have prayed since "then." Praise God forever.

I want to personally encourage each reader to remember that while mistakes will always happen (and you cannot stop others from reminding you of them), prayer will always uplift and comfort you. Reminders are everywhere. Take television news: even if the discussion is about something good a person has done, the announcer typically reminds us of that person's past mistakes, regardless of how long ago they were made. For example, whenever there is an update on Tiger Wood's recovery from his back injury, the announcer also notes that Tiger failed years ago when he was caught having sexual activities with several women. What does that have to do with his injured back? Nothing! You see what I am saying? There will always be someone to remind you of your mistakes. I encourage you to pray – and to remind yourself that you have prayed since "then."

Hey, here is another example from the Bible, from the account of the thief on the cross in **Luke 23:39-43**:

(39) One of the criminals who was suspended kept up a railing at Him,

saying, Are You not the Christ (the Messiah)? Rescue yourself and us [from death]! (40) But the other one reproved him, saying Do you not even fear God, seeing you yourself are under the same sentence of condemnation and suffering the same penalty? (41) And we indeed suffer it justly, receiving the due reward of our actions; but this Man has done nothing out of the way [nothing strange or eccentric or perverse or unreasonable]. (42) Then he said to Jesus, Lord, remember me when You come in Your kingly glory! (43) And He answered him, Truly I tell you, today you shall be with me in Paradise.

What? Jesus did not remind the thief of all the mistakes he had made. No, **not one time** did Jesus condemn this man. On the contrary, He welcomed him into the kingdom. Oh my, I pray that you, dear reader, will carefully consider this lesson, because if Jesus had a heart like this, then we can too. God's Holy Spirit will come to our aid in helping others come into the kingdom - but we will not bring them in by condemnation and constant reminders of their mistakes. Let me say, we can do the works Jesus did. However, that may mean that we need to stop looking at His works as unattainable miracles and start loving and forgiving like Him! I believe loving and forgiving are great works and certainly are miracles, but they are works and miracles we as individuals can manifest. If we can look beyond the mistakes we experience to love and forgive ourselves and others, what a miracle that will be!

I understand that reminding people of their mistakes is nothing new. We read about the thief on the cross, but what about Apostle Paul who wrote the majority of the New Testament? It would take too much space to write the Scriptures out, so I encourage you to please read all of **Acts chapters 8 and 9.** I will provide a summarized snippet.

Paul was a very knowledgeable man in things pertaining to the law of Moses. His actions were strictly based on his interpretation of Scripture. He was committed to fulfilling the law and viewed the followers of Jesus as people who were opposing the law. As a result, he treated them terribly and laid waste to their church. The Bible indicates that he dragged men and women out of worship and committed them to prison. What a mistake - and all because that is where he was at the time.

We later read that Jesus informed His servant, Ananias, that Paul was the chosen instrument that He would use to minister to the Gentiles. Ananias' immediate response was to remind God of what Paul had done (his "then"). Isn't this Jesus who is talking to Ananias? Can we not hypothesize that God knew about Paul's mistakes **when He called him?** It is one thing to remind humans of the past, but to **remind God?** Oh yes, we probably do this more than we realize. We often reject the one whom God has sent as if God did not know what He was doing. I believe it is safe to say that God knew quite a bit about Paul's past, just as He does ours.

I know, from studying the Scriptures, that Paul became a person of prayer and sought to understand God and His Word. I believe **2 Corinthians 7:2** was his way of saying I have prayed since "then."

> Do open your hearts to us again [enlarge them to take us in]. We have wronged no one, we have betrayed or corrupted no one, we have cheated or taken advantage of no one.

I consider his statement the fruit of prayer. I know from my own experiences that it is easy to live with guilt over your mistakes. But I believe Paul, like me, had to let the past go to fulfill his destiny. He could not allow himself or others to keep him in his "thens" if he was going to truly serve God. I thank God for prayer.

I want to share more about prayer and its' benefits. Let us look at **Matthew 14:23-29** that reads:

(23) And after He had dismissed the multitudes, He went up into the hills by Himself to pray. When it was evening, He was still there alone. (24) But the boat was by this time out on the sea, many furlongs [a furlong is one-eighth of a mile] distant from the land, beaten and tossed by the waves, for the wind was against them. (25) And in the fourth watch [between 3:00 – 6:00 A.M.] of the night, Jesus came to them, walking on the sea. (26) And when the disciples saw Him walking on the sea, they were terrified and said, It is a ghost! And they screamed out with fright. (27) But instantly He spoke to them, saying, Take courage! I AM! Stop being afraid! (28) And Peter answered Him, Lord, if it is You, command me to come to You on the water. (29) He said, Come! So, Peter got out of the boat and walked on the water, and he came toward Jesus.

There is a note in the Dake's Annotated Reference Bible that speaks to my heart on this Scripture:

> "Alone with God in retirement from the world and in prayer and meditation, as He so often was. His private praying and conquest of Satan were the secret of His public power. It was by prayer that He received the Holy Spirit. It was by continued prayer that He received fresh anointings of the Spirit for His daily work. He used the same methods to get and keep power that are required of believers."

I recall when I first read this perspective because it confirmed what the Holy Spirit had revealed to me about the benefits of prayer, specifically the power "to do" because of prayer and, most importantly, how we are able to receive more of the Holy Spirit via prayer.

If we are truthful, we can admit that we want results when we pray. We have the promises of God but must settle in our hearts that we will not receive them by doing things our way. I believe it is important that the likeness of Christ is revealed in every believer. He must constitute all that we do. I can assure you that such grace does not come without a great price, but it can be attained by our steadfastness to surrender totally to the Head of the Church, Christ Jesus.

Our surrendering must be in every area and relationship. I am reminded of **John 5:30** that reads:

> I am able to do nothing from Myself [independently, of My own accord – but only as I am taught by God and as I get His orders]. Even as I hear, I judge [I decide as I am bidden to decide. As the voice comes to Me, so I give a decision], and My judgment is right (just, righteous), because I do not seek or consult My own will [I have no desire to do what is pleasing to Myself, My own aim, My own purpose] but only the will and pleasure of the Father Who sent Me.

I believe this should be the attitude of every believer. If we are not living like Christ – in mercy, love, forgiveness, humility, etc., - then our past, present, and future labor and prayers will be in vain.

Are you ready to see others healed emotionally, physically, and spiritually? Are you ready to heal and have your prayers answered? I pray I have provided some insight on how that can occur in your life. Many years ago, my husband said, "A man with an experience is not at the mercy of a man with an argument." I have since heard others use this phrase as well. What I am sharing in this book is out of my experience. I came to a point in my life where I was tired of praying with no results. I also considered what the Scriptures said about righteousness (conformity to God's way in purposes, thoughts, and actions). I made it my purpose to allow the Holy Spirit to live in my heart constantly and to do His work inside of me.

It was the Holy Spirit who I heard saying "You have prayed since "then" in my spirit when I was constantly and endlessly being reminded of my mistakes - by others as well as my own thinking. I lived for a long time with a repetitive internal voice that said I was inadequate because of my mistakes. I have since felt a freedom inside that was and is ineffable. I have learned to remember and express that statement whenever I am – or others are - influenced by the enemy to bring back painful memories that I cannot change. Through prayer, we can escape what I call the age-old feeling of living with guilt.

Many individuals have lived with guilt for years. It could be due to a failed marriage or the way you raised your children or any number of things; regardless, you made mistakes. You did what you did or said what you said because that was where you were at the time. I know how you feel, but you do not have to stay in a place of guilt.

Below is a brief list of the consequences of my living with guilt:

- I sought the approval of others.
- I provided financial resources to prove my love.
- I accepted blame for mistakes I hadn't made to be accepted (see next chapter).
- I delayed my Divine destiny.
- I explained my actions when explaining was unnecessary.
- I felt inadequate whenever I was misunderstood.
- I put confidence in people rather than God.
- I felt I deserved all punishment that came my way.
- I lived as a hypocrite because the truth was too painful to admit.

My dear reader, I could list other consequences, but these were the worst. I lived as a saved person for most of my life. However, the day came that - when I was at the highest height of pain - I surrendered all of me to God. I knew I couldn't go on as I was. It was through prayer and meditating upon the Word of God, that freedom began to ring in my life. I began to experience that some-one greater than me and my problems was inside of me.

The Holy Spirit led me to the following Scriptures that cata-pulted me to freedom and a release from my past mistakes (my "thens"):

### Luke 9:62)

Jesus said to him, No one who puts his hand to the plow and looks back [to the things behind] is fit for the kingdom of God.

### (John 3:20-22)

[20] Whenever our hearts in [tormenting] self-accusation make us feel guilty and condemn us, [For we are in God's hands.] For He is above and greater than our consciences (our hearts), and He knows (perceives and understands) everything [nothing is hidden from Him]. [21] And, beloved, if our consciences (our hearts) do not accuse us [if they do not make us feel guilty and condemn us], we have confidence (complete assurance and boldness) before God, [22] And we receive from Him whatever we ask, because we [watchfully] obey His orders [observe His suggestions and injunctions, follow His plan for us] and [habitually] practice what is pleasing to Him.

I encourage you to stop looking back at your mistakes and choose to walk in the freedom that God has provided. Stop allowing yourself or others to keep you in bondage with things you cannot change. Jesus' death, burial, and resurrection broke our chains and removed our shackles. I can't express enough the importance of believing, receiving, and applying what He did in your life. These actions led to a radical transformation in my life.

I want you to experience the same transformation. I pray God's blessing on you on your new journey of freedom.

# FALSE GUILT

"Now who is there to hurt you if you are zealous followers of that which is good? (14) But even in case you should suffer for the sake of righteousness, [you are] blessed (happy, to be envied). Do not dread or be afraid of their threats, nor be disturbed [by their opposition]. (15) But in your hearts set Christ apart as holy [and acknowledge Him] as Lord. Always be ready to give a logical defense to anyone who asks you to account for the hope that is in you, but do it courteously and respectfully. (16) [And see to it that] your conscience is entirely clear (unimpaired), so that, when you are falsely accused as evildoers, those who threaten you abusively and revile your right behavior in Christ may come to be ashamed [of slandering your good lives]. (17) For [it is] better to suffer [unjustly] for doing right, if that should be God's will, than to suffer [justly] for doing wrong."
**(I Peter 3:14-17)**

U p to this point, I have focused on the "thens" that we have committed in our lives. But what about the "thens" that we did not commit but for which we feel guilty? I think we need to discuss those as well.

I define false guilt as guilt projected on us by those who refuse to be responsible and accountable. This guilt normally comes from people whom we have emotional connections such as family, friends, close associates and even colleagues at work. Such emotional connections can open the door for people to project guilt upon others with whom they are connected. False guilt is unlike true guilt in that you are innocent of wrongdoing - yet you may still feel guilty.

I must be honest with you, false guilt - like true guilt - comes from not being free. False guilt takes advantage of love via people who avoid being responsible for themselves. Oh, how many of you have experienced this (or are experiencing it right now)?

I have had family members who refused to see the truth about themselves and blamed me for their circumstances. I was once summoned to a family picnic and quickly realized that I was summoned to face the judges. The family present at this event accused me of not participating in family activities. I felt like I was sitting in a courtroom before a jury that had found me guilty without hearing my defense. I started a rebuttal but decided to leave. However, although I may have seemed strong as I left, I walked away feeling guilty. I wondered what else I could do or could have done to prove my love for them?

I hope you noticed the word "prove" above, because proving seems to link with both true and false guilt; it, too, is associated with not being free. I am convinced that freedom is critical to living victoriously. Before that picnic, there had been many occasions when I didn't know of certain family gatherings or a family member informed me about an event at the last minute. Also, I felt that my family had not supported me as an individual. Yes, I found myself feeling guilty – but this was false guilt, based on Momma's words to my childhood self which I now know were not true. I love my family, but I should not have to suffer to prove that love. I recall one of my kids saying "Momma, I remember when you would have your family over to try and bring peace, but it was always a problem so you finally stopped."

At that time in my life, I willingly took on the guilt and the responsibility for my family's disappointment. Because family is family, we tend to assume that we must do something to bring about change, even when our relatives are demonstrating that they do not want change or be held responsible and accountable for their role in the relationship. False guilt! God help us!

I have, of course, made mistakes as a sister, wife, mother, and friend. However, I have learned that people tend to project their guilt on you when they know how much you care. They know that this projection will cause you to do for them when you shouldn't. I experienced others' projections for so long that I started to believe I was guilty when I was innocent. There is a difference between true and false guilt, you know!

As a sister, wife, mother, and friend, I did many things to prove my love, but my proving was to no avail because "proving" was not what was needed. I was and am responsible for me, and others were and are responsible for themselves. It is one thing to be guilty and hurt, but another to not be guilty and nonetheless carry the burden. That is not the will of God. I am thankful that I finally came to that realization.

I confess that it took me a long time to come to that realization because of the many mistakes I had made. Like me, you may encounter family members who say they forgive you but who continue to remind you of your past or choose not to have a relationship with you; these actions do not represent forgiveness according to God's Word (I will discuss forgiveness in the next chapter).

False guilt seems to be more easily accepted when it involves our loved ones. While there are complex reasons for this phenomenon, it is certainly in part because we care; it also occurs because we are inclined to give them the benefit of the doubt. For example, some of my family members exaggerated or lied about past situations. I am not referring to sharing an opinion about something that happened in the past, but rather about deliberately making false statements about me or our experience together. I experienced living in false guilt for years because of my desire to "prove" I was worthy of love by having an intimate relationship with certain of my family members in this context. As stated prior, "proving" was not what was needed. I believe – based on God's Word – what was needed was love, the truth, and forgiveness – all tools necessary to move forward in a real relationship.

As you know real relationships take more than one person's contributions - and both parties must have the same desire and intention to move forward. And you can't force anyone to be with you, forgive you or do anything conducive to a healthy relationship. If you struggle with false guilt, I encourage you to rest in God's peace knowing that you have done your part to contribute to a healthy relationship. In this way, you can choose not to live with the false guilt. Please remember, dear reader, regardless if it is true guilt or false guilt to confess your mantra – I have prayed since "then."

Let's look at another example. I recently had a conversation with a precious lady who had chosen to use all her monetary resources for her child. Her child had been in and out of jail, taking no responsibility for self. She cried as she shared how she could have been free of debt, but her child needed her more. She was also facing the possibility of losing her home. My heart broke because of my own experiences of doing crazy things for loved ones because of false guilt. She discussed how she had to keep helping because she was a mother. Her child knew the depths of her love and projected guilt on her. Sadly, she received and took on that false guilt, despite having done nothing to cause the child to continue to choose a life of crime. Unfortunately, however, she was — through her heartfelt and best-intentioned efforts - promoting a sense of entitlement.

I walked away wishing I could have spoken to her about true and false guilt, but her posture was such that I realized it was not the right time to share. It was her child, and she would continue to help. Hey, been there and done that but I HAVE PRAYED SINCE "THEN." I pray that the Holy Spirit will reach her as He reached me so that she can be free of this false guilt. I pray to see her someday and hear her testimony of being radically changed because of prayer and understanding God's Word. I would love to hear her say "I have prayed since then." Praise God always. My experiences of true and false guilt empowered me to show her mercy and not condemnation. I can pray; I can intercede; I do not always have to talk!

# FORGIVENESS

(14) For if you forgive people their trespasses [their reckless and willful sins, leaving them, letting them go, and giving up resentment], your heavenly Father will also forgive you. (15) But if you do not forgive others their trespasses [their reckless and willful sins, leaving them, letting them go, and giving up resentment], neither will your Father forgive you your trespasses.

**(Matthew 6:14-15)**

(3) Pay attention and always be on your guard [looking out for one another]. If your brother sins (misses the mark), solemnly tell him so and reprove him, and if he repents (feels sorry for having sinned), forgive him. (4) And even if he sins against you seven times in a day, and turns to you seven times and says, I repent [I am sorry], you must forgive him (give up resentment and consider the offense as recalled and annulled).

**(Luke 17:3-4)**

Dear reader, there have been times when God has forgiven me at least seven times in a day. Knowing this, I can't imagine not forgiving anyone, regardless of the mistake(s) they may have made. Because of prayer and God's Word, I forgave my mother; I forgave my husband and he forgave me. We both realized that we had fallen short of God's glory and chose to not stay in the past, constantly reminding each other of our failures.

In writing about both true and false guilt, I shared how I asked for and received forgiveness from family and friends. Yet the actions of some of those who said they forgave me did not reflect forgiveness. How can we forgive and remain separated, choosing not to engage in dialogue with one another? Because I had learned God's definition of forgiveness, it seemed to me that relationships could start fresh and build into something beautiful. According to God's Word, our mistake(s) should be forgiven and forgotten. I practically begged one of my family members to forgive me; the response was "I forgive you, but there will not be a relationship." This individual also confesses to be a believer in Christ. Please excuse me, but I believe the Scriptures are clear that we are to forgive as if there was never a mistake. Forgiveness is so important to God that He will not forgive us until we forgive others. I believe we manifest self-righteousness when we can't forgive and move forward in unity and love.

I want to provide another Scripture that I believe will empower you to walk in forgiveness:

**(Matthew 5:13-16)**
[13] You are the salt of the earth, but if the salt has lost its taste (its strength, its quality), how can its saltness be restored? It is not good for anything any longer but to be thrown out and trodden underfoot by men.

(14) You are the light of the world. A city set on a hill cannot be hidden. (15) Nor do men light a lamp and put it under a peck measure, but on a lampstand, and it gives light to all in the house. (16) Let your light so shine before men that they may see your moral excellence and your praiseworthy, noble, and good deeds and recognize and honor and praise and glorify your Father Who is in heaven.

If you have struggled to forgive others or are struggling now, please declare these words:

## I AM THE SALT OF THE EARTH.
## I AM THE LIGHT OF THE WORLD.

You are taking responsibility for yourself and your life in Christ. More importantly, you will demonstrate God's love to others so that perhaps their non-forgiving now may eventually become their "then." As I stated previously, God has forgiven me at least seven times in a day (probably more – lol) – His forgiveness was salt and light to my soul because often I knew I probably didn't deserve forgiveness for the deliberate things I did or said. Hey, I am just real with you. I believe that the words **forgive** and **deserve** are mutually exclusive. Guess what? This is one of the many things I love about God; He doesn't focus on if we deserve anything. He is all about the love that **gives** and the love that sets **free**.

I encourage you to find a way to forgive even those who are incapable of enjoying and sharing God's forgiveness. You do this by "being" the salt and the light! Praise God forever.

You know I like to give examples (my experiences). I recall many years ago while in prayer that I sensed the need to go to my Momma and ask her to forgive me for whatever hurt I caused as a child. I promise, this made no sense to me because she was the Momma who abandoned me; I was the child! I recall how strongly I felt the need to go so I surrendered and went. I was really expecting Momma to say "baby, I need to ask you to forgive me" but she didn't - quite the contrary - Momma said, "I forgive you honey."

I realized that Momma wasn't capable of asking me to forgive her – at least she knew I didn't hold anything against her because I asked her to forgive me. At that moment, I believe I went from a burden to a benefit – a benefit of learning to forgive whether it is deserved or not and being responsible for my life and growth in Christ. Momma appeared to be happy that I asked her to forgive me. I didn't know at the time, but I was being the salt and the light and I was o.k. with Momma's appearance of happiness.

Finally, please remember that while we were sinners, totally **against** God, He sent His only begotten son to suffer and die for us – all because He loved us. I can't add anything to that!

# RISE AND SHINE

(17) And when they had brought them forth, they said, Escape for your life! Do not look behind you or stop anywhere in the whole valley; escape to the mountains [of Moab], lest you be consumed. (26) But [Lot's] wife looked back from behind him, and she became a pillar of salt.
**(Genesis 19:17 and 26)**

Arise [from the depression and prostration in which circumstances have kept you – rise to a new life]! Shine (be radiant with the glory of the Lord), for your light has come, and the glory of the Lord has risen upon you!
**(Isaiah 60:1)**

For the rest, brethren, whatever is true, whatever is worthy of reverence and is honorable and seemly, whatever is just, whatever is pure, whatever is lovely and lovable, whatever is kind and winsome and gracious, if there is any virtue and excellence, if there is anything worthy of praise, think on and weigh and take account of these things [fix your minds on them.]
**(Philippians 4:8)**

The day came when I heard the words "rise and shine" in my spirit. However, as encouraged as I was hearing them, I did not know how to rise and shine.

Like a ship that cannot move forward as long as it is anchored, I was being held back by both true and false guilt. I wanted to rise and shine and fulfill my destiny but struggled to let go. I didn't realize the depth of my wanting to prove Momma wrong. And my constant efforts toward proving caused me to hold on to people and thoughts that only caused unhappiness and unfruitfulness in my life.

I knew the mistakes I had made - and those I had not made - so why stay anchored? I ask you, have you ever tried letting go? It is not such an easy task! I wasn't as free as I supposed I was. Jesus said the truth would make us free; He didn't say it wouldn't hurt. I didn't want to accept the possibility of not being connected to those whom I loved. I learned that removing the anchor of the past does not always mean a physical separation, but it does often entail an emotional one. I had to accept the things I could not change, and God never asked me to change other people, only myself.

I had to see the truth, the whole truth and nothing but the truth if I was going to be free. I had to learn to manage every hurtful situation from a Biblical perspective. I needed to detach my emotions from everyone and everything that I allowed to hinder me. I had to choose to obey Philippians 4:8.

The extensive energy I had customarily spent holding on to guilt had to be given to letting go in order to move forward. I didn't want to continue **talking** about my destiny or how great God was and is. I wanted to **experience** these so that others could bear witness and experience them as well. My first step was writing this book.

I confess that occasionally I have allowed my ship to slow

down because of my emotions. However, each time, God rescued me – and He continues to rescue me by reminding me of His love. More importantly, He reminds me that I have been my own worst enemy when making choices that were not healthy or beneficial to His kingdom.

I believe there are three primary indications of having let go:

- You immediately recognize the enemy's attempts to use true and false guilt against you.
- You do not need to contact your best friend to talk about the situation.
- God becomes your best friend forever.

I encourage you to rise and shine. Please accept God's forgiveness for yourself and others. Pray for them to be free and experience God's love and mercy as you have. It works - I promise. I also want to tell you that you may lose some family and friends as you walk in your freedom, but you will be alright (it took me a long time to accept this truth). What God has for you is far greater than any loss you may encounter. And **always** remember this:

**(John 8:36)**
So, if the Son liberates you [makes you free men],
then you are really and unquestionably free.

**The chains are broken and the shackles removed!
It is time to live without guilt through the power of
prayer!**

# PERSONAL PRAYER
# TESTAMENTS

I want to share others "thens" with you and to demonstrate how prayer impacted their lives. It is my prayer that you will be encouraged by their testimony. I call them "prayers" to protect their privacy.

## Prayer #1

My experience is that, because of growing up in financial lack; I carried feelings of rejection which grew deeper throughout my life. As a result, I held my pain inside and reacted much of the time in anger. I regret releasing anger when I was hurt, which many times hurt others and left me with feelings of regret.

Through prayer, God encouraged me and gave me hope and faith that He heard me, saw me, and would provide what I needed to see and receive my answer.

By hearing God's words, I came to understand that it was not others causing my hurt, but myself. I was not aligning my thinking and actions with the Word of God. By hearing the truth of God's Word, I came to understand my identity in Christ. I started renewing my mind and walking by the truth found in His Word. I chose to receive the Word of God and be transformed into my true identity, which is the image of Christ.

## Prayer #2

The experience I would like to share is my past addiction. My experience of addiction was more than overwhelming. It was catastrophic. I lost family, friends, and other loved ones. I managed to acquire a small fortune through my many misdeeds as I embarked on a life of crime to support my addictive lifestyle of misery and a lot of regrets. I saw myself as others saw me: as having great potential but no willpower to break free. When I finally found the courage to try to break free, I failed because my expectation of freedom was from the hand of man rather than from the hand of God. I became a part of a local assembly that preached the Word of God, and I received Jesus as Lord of my life. I still carried a feeling of guilt because of my many "thens."

I was empowered through prayer in my inner man to move forward in the things of God. I believe prayer strengthened me in mind, body, and spirit. As a result, I have changed the way I see things. I do not allow my "thens" to control my life.

I took other steps such as continually renewing my mind to the Word of God and get involved in my local assembly. Because of my "thens" I have compassion for others who struggle with addiction. I have become involved in community groups to help others with their "thens."

## Prayer #3

I had a habit of running and pointing the finger at others and not taking responsibility for myself. I carried a feeling of guilt all the time and blamed others for this feeling. It was because of my upbringing that I felt a sense of worthlessness. My "then" experiences caused me to say a lot of things that were mean and to do a lot of things without regard for others. I only knew to blame others because of the hurt I carried inside. It was my way of protecting myself. I was known as a mean person, even though in my heart, I did care.

I began to talk to God, sharing how I felt inside. I knew I had caused the label of meanness but didn't know how to change. It seemed that my "thens" were too much for a change, even if it was from God. I continued to pray and open my heart to Him, and one day, I finally experienced a new freedom. He does care about me.

He did forgive me for my "thens." I realized that I needed to forgive myself and start treating people the way He wanted me to and that was with love. I started and continued to experience others seeing me differently. I believe prayer conquered my "thens" and I am so glad.

I decided never to run again. I am taking responsibility for my actions and staying connected to Christ and His Word. I am determined to be a doer of His Word and not a talker.

## Prayer #4

A pattern of behavior that I truly regret and caused me to live with guilt for many years was the desire to have a spouse in my life. I made many mistakes that caused me to live in lack, shame, and low self-esteem. I caused hurt also to others for whom I was responsible.

The change came in my life as I started to learn about Jesus and His Word. I started to pray and seek Him for myself. He revealed that He knew what things I needed, including my desire to have a spouse. There was nothing wrong with wanting marriage, but my desire overrode my doing things the right way. I started learning more about God and found myself falling deeper in love with Him. I learned the power of prayer to reveal deep truths in my heart and to set me free. Because of my prayer life, I learned the difference between flesh and spirit and between need and want.

I took additional steps by getting Godly counseling before making decisions. I have grown and overcome my "thens" because of consistent prayer, study, and application of God's Word.

## Prayer #5

I used to be a person that would try and help EVERYONE. I used to be a person to fix everything. I would overextend myself in many areas because I would not say "no" or even check my schedule or circumstances to see if the request was feasible for my family and me. I would do things for people over and over, even if they did not return the favor. Sometimes people viewed me as overbearing and controlling because I "helped" even when not asked.

Because I am a believer, I started to pray and ask God the reasons I did these things. I cried out for help because of the label (or, as Pastor Ruth calls them, "thens.") Through prayer, God revealed to me that because I was the oldest child and my divorced mom relied heavily on me to care for my brother and to pick up the slack when she had to work, I took on the "I can fix it" behavior. No one needed to ask; I just did what was needed. My "then" may have worked for my mom and brother, but it did not for others. It was painful to experience others being frustrated and saying I was overbearing. I had no balance; I just wanted to help because I loved people. As I continued to pray, God came to my aid. He began to reveal truths to me that were hard to accept. For example, my mother never liked seeing things as they were and that is why I didn't want to accept the labels others put on me, even though I was causing them. I didn't want to see that truth. But because of prayer, I chose to and honestly received my freedom.

As a prayer, I have learned to say "no" without feeling guilty. I no longer feel pressured to be the "fixer." I have learned to seek God's will before doing or saying things. I am also able to adjust to ensure that I am not involved in "unequally yoked" relationships. Because of prayer, I can now see the truth about myself and others.

## Prayer #6

I always felt I had a laid-back personality because of the "good time" mindset I used to have. I always wondered why people

75

would ignore things I said or not give me opportunities to handle serious or complex situations. A little background about me: I love playing and having a good time. Growing up, I used to wake up early and watch the Hanna-Barbera and Looney Tunes cartoons. In my family, everyone was always enjoying themselves. Even through tragedy, everyone found ways to find excitement, and that impacted how I saw life. I would look for excitement in everything I did, even in inappropriate situations. This "good time" attitude/behavior caused me to get into trouble at school, not because I was disrespectful, but because I was playing when I should have been paying attention. All I wanted to do was have fun and enjoy life. That was the most important thing to me. The way I saw it, I was not hurting anyone; What's wrong with wanting to smile and have a "good time?" I wasn't doing drugs, breaking the law, or bringing shame to my family name, so how could anyone have a problem with the way I acted?

As an adult, this "good time" mindset caused people not to take me seriously. Even though I was knowledgeable in areas and possibly had the answer(s) people needed, they didn't want to come to me because of the constant joking I did. This behavior caused issues in different areas of my life. One area is my marriage. My wife finally confided in me that she didn't completely trust me. Even though I did a lot of the right things, she was always afraid I was going to do or say something that would embarrass her, causing her to not fully open her heart to me. In turn, I felt disconnected from her because of her holding back. I tried taking matters into my own hands to solve our issues, but my "good time" view on life never changed causing her to not trust me; this caused us to go in a never-ending cycle. We would have great periods of times but eventually would end back in unhappiness. Honestly, I wasn't sure if our marriage would last.

I admit that this isn't as big as some "thens" like adultery or abuse, and many people would say "What's the big deal?" But my "then" was a big deal from my wife's perspective. My "then" almost cost me my marriage.

Through prayer, the Holy Spirit was able to give me the strength to start a journey of looking at things differently. I confess that - because I was doing so many things right - realizing I needed to change was no small task. I even wish I could share that it was overnight, but it wasn't. I can say that, through prayer, the Holy Spirit chipped away at my heart and revealed how my "good time" mindset was a contributing factor to my wife's and my experiences. Because of prayer, both of us began to see what we needed to change to be a better spouse. But this is my story.

As I think about other steps I took to move forward and live a guilt-free life, I am reminded of how I finally came to a place of not being reluctant to open my heart fully to God. I didn't want to give Him a part of me, but all of me. My journey became more empowering because of prayer. My trust in God became stronger and my ability to hear His voice was greatly increasing. My wife began to open her heart to me; she began to trust me. Our marriage is stronger than ever. My "then" is not my "now." I am thankful to God for His patience with me.

Dear reader: I pray these stories have encouraged you to give your "thens" to God in prayer. Perhaps you may have seen yourself in one of them. If so, I believe you also see the solution.

# CONCLUSION

I lived with true and false guilt most of my life. I apologized to those whom I knowingly hurt. My foundation caused me to behave in a needy fashion and constantly try to prove myself when proving wasn't necessary. It is no small task to let go of true guilt - especially when it involves your family, particularly your children. However, I finally realized that I couldn't change my past and that holding on to the past was delaying my destiny. My deliverance and freedom began when I learned about Jesus and His love for me. I started to pray; pouring my heart out to Him and allowing His Spirit to speak to my spirit. I will forever cherish my mantra "I have prayed since then." The understanding of His Word and prayer will forever be in my life's toolkit.

I have learned that no matter how profound my growth is in Christ, there will always be a messenger used by the enemy to remind me of the past. More importantly, though, I have learned the tremendous power of having a lifestyle of prayer, meditation, and obeying God's Word.

I continue to experience that weapons may be formed but with God's love and prayer they do not become manifest in my life. We can form weapons by holding onto our "thens" and accepting the reminders of them from others. Or we can choose to do better. As my own history with my mother and family and the life stories in the testaments chapter show, the power lies inside of us to let go by embracing a lifestyle of prayer. If we can do so, others will eventually experience us as new people.

I stress that your future is your responsibility alone. Therefore, choose to be responsible and accountable for making decisions from a Biblical perspective.

I pray my story and the others above will inspire you to

start a new journey in life. I believe in you. More importantly, God believes in you! Arise and be free!

### (Psalms 23:6)

Surely or only goodness, mercy, and unfailing love shall follow me all the days of my life, and through the length of my days the house of the Lord [and His presence] shall be my dwelling place.

### (2 Corinthians 5:17)

Therefore, if any person is [ingrafted] in Christ (the Messiah) he is a new creation (a new creature altogether); the old [previous moral and spiritual condition] has passed away. Behold, the fresh and new has come!

### PRAISE GOD FOREVER!

Thanks for taking the time to read my story.
I love each of you.

Made in the USA
Columbia, SC
08 April 2019